# Introverts

# Embrace the Gift of an Introverted Mind and Lead a Life Full of Success

# Table of Contents

# Introduction

I want to thank you and congratulate you for purchasing the book, "Introverts: Embrace the Gift of an Introverted Mind and Lead a Life Full of Success."

No one is purely extrovert or entirely introvert. Everyone in some way falls in one of the spaces between extreme extroversion and introversion. Every now and then, you become inclined to one side more than the other. Once and a while, it's the other way around. But the real issue is not about the labels. It's how you use both sides of your personality as an advantage in becoming successful.

In this book, you'll find hidden talents that you might have by learning how to look inside of you. This book will help you merge the world of introversion in the current extroverted world you live. It will help you understand the true meaning of being an introvert. It will also show you how you can use your introvert side to become successful. The strategies presented here are applicable no matter what your passions in life are.

Whether you are dominantly extroverted or introverted, this book will reveal many things about you. Unleash the power of introversion and witness the marvelous things you once thought you could not do!

Thanks again for purchasing this book, I hope you enjoy it!

*"Yesterday is a kid in the corner*
*Yesterday is dead end over*
*Don't close your eyes*
*This is your life*
*Are you who you want to be?*
*Is it everything you dreamed it would be?"*

*This is Your Life, Switchfoot*

# Chapter 1 - Are you an Introvert?

"There are two distinct groups of people in the world: the ones who tell stories and those who pay attention"

—Daniel Goncalves

Have you ever wondered why the world of social media seems much more glamorous than the real world?Social media isn't for communication anymore. On a fast-paced outgrowth of time, it became a place for people's inner selves. Social media has become the safe haven for introverts and another interaction platform for extroverts.

It indeed brought the worlds of introverts and extroverts close yet far away. What are introverts and extroverts, anyway?

## THE EXTROVERT FACTION

Extroverts are people who find being alonemind numbing. If you put them in a waiting area,you'll find them reaching for their phones, looking for someone to talk to. Their phones are like their lifelines to other people. These people can't live a day without talking to someone. If you do not see them busy with their social media accounts, you'll spot them striking a conversation withthe stranger beside them.

Extroverts frequently spend their free time doing activities with their group of friends.

In fact, they consider their home as a place for everybody to have fun. They find friends to make sure they won't walk this earth alone. For them, going out is blending in with the crowds;being in the middle of constant chatter, cluttered noises and food.

They regard their co-extroverts as nice, outgoing people who won't surprise them with weird stuff. However, they are careful being around introverts because they see them as moody creatures who only like to read and be by themselves.

## THE INTROVERT FACTION

Introverts are people who enjoy alone time. They love the peace it gives them. A long waiting line is never a problem as long as they have a bookworth reading in their hands. For them, books are low-cost means of travel, having an adventure, and meeting fascinating people.

Reading books gives them a sense of comfort by being lost in its pages. They usually use their free time reading without breaks until they're in danger of going blind. In fact, hunger can't even stop them sometimes.

Introverts refer to friends as folks who understand when they need to be alone. For them, hanging out is having stimulating discussions with a close friend or two. Mostly, they go out to see a band, a play, a movie and drink cups of coffee. They define love as someone appreciating and understanding them.

They find their co-introverts as people who show perfectly natural limitation and attention when meeting new people. They define introverts as people who enjoy solitude and find philosophical turn of mind pleasurable.

However, they find extroverts as boisterous people who are undeniably nice and fun. However, being around extroverts sap introverts of energy because of the unnecessary noises, high levels of energy, and unpredictable bursts of laughter.

# INTROVERT/EXTROVERT TEST

Can you consider yourself under one of those two factions? Or are you a little confused? For you to be more certain whether you're an extrovert or introvert, here is a quick test for you. Simply answer these questions with an honest Yes or No. Don't answer "sometimes" or "maybe" to understand this test better.

- Do you prefer one-on-one conversations rather than group discussions?

- Are you a good listener?

- Can you express yourself more in writing?

- Are you afraid of taking big risks?

- Are you uncomfortable with conflicts?

- Can you focus more on your work if you are alone?

- Do you prefer showing your work only when it's already finished?

- Do you take your time to think first before speaking, responding or replying to someone?

- Do you find random or unexpected calls terrifying?

- Do you find yourself at a loss for words when you get an unexpected phone call?

- Would you rather stay at home during the weekends?

- Do you find multi-tasking extra difficult or unnatural?

- Do you prefer celebrating your birthdays with a small group of people rather than throw a huge party?

## WEIGHING YOUR INTROVERTED SIDE

Extroverts are people who focus more on the outside world. They usually draw their energy from social interactions; they also like collaborating with others. They do not like being alone for extended amounts of time; they find it draining. On the other hand, introverts focus more on their internal world. They engage more on thought journeys than the physical ones. They draw energy by gaining ideas and spending time alone.

If you answered "no" to most of the questions stated above, then you're most likely an extrovert. If you answered "yes" to more questions, then you're probably an introvert. However, no matter which side is dominant, the point is there is always an introverted side in everybody. The main purpose of this book is for you to recognize that. The gift of introversion longs for your attention.

## So Close Yet So Far

Technology indeed brought massive development to the world. It brought people closer—perhaps virtually—but it still didn't fill the void in everyone's heart. The void that longs for deep and wide internal connection is still missing. But technology is not the one to blame; it's the age-old belief that you can only get this kind of connection throuh face-to-face interactions.

*"Open my mouth*
*All that comes out*
*Are white noise*
*And incomprehensible sounds*
*But all you ever do*
*Is turn me down"*


*White Noise, Pvris*

# Chapter 2 - The Forgotten Identity

*"Our culture made a virtue of living only as extroverts. We discouraged the inner journey, the quest for a center. So we lost our center and have to find it again."*

*—Anais Nin*

The term *extrovert* and *introvert* came from the16 Myers-Briggs Personalities. It is a kind of personality test that tells how people relate with other people (Introvert/Extrovert), how they take in information (Sensing/Intuition), manage decisions (Thinking/Feeling) and organize their selves (Judging/Perceiving).

Extroversion and introversion is one of the Myers-Briggs Type Indicator (MBTI), a test that shows a person's preferred means of interacting with the world. Carl Jung, a famous Swiss psychiatrist, defined extroverts as action-oriented people who prefer interacting with others. In contrast, he defined introverts as reflective thinkers who need tranquility to regain their energy.

## REDEFINING WHAT BEING AN INTROVERT MEANS

Introvert and extroverts are far beyond being opposite forces. Both have their own special strength and weaknesses. However, introverts are more misunderstood in the society today. So here is a list of society's impression on introverts versus who they actually are.

## Weird vs. Quirky

What most extroverts think about introverts is that they are weird, mainly because they do things differently. Introverts always challengethemselves to go beyond the norm, but it doesn't mean they're twisted lunatics.

The definition of fun is simply riding their train of thought. Their quirks help them keep track of their progress. In fact, their natural quirkiness is actually what makes them cute.

## Mute vs. Selective in Speaking

Maybe the reason why the world doesn't notice the beauty of introversion is the fact introverts tend to be quiet. They always keep their thoughts to themselves. Or otherwise, it's on their journals, diaries or blogs. But it doesn't necessarily mean that they're mute.

No, introverts are not mute. They just prefer to think long and hard before they open their mouths. They listen carefully before saying something to contribute to the conversation. If they don't find the topic of the conversation interesting, they wouldn't speak, but they would always be listening. They don't like to talk just for the sake of talking. They always yearn for meaningful and creative moments. Talk to them about something they find fascinating and you can be sure that they would be talking for hours.

## Rude vs. Real

In a world that always aim to please, being real and honest can be tough. Typical people would put on a mask just to gain society's acceptance, but many introverts aren't like that. They prefer to be real and honest,but society finds it rude. Most introverts find this behavior of society tiring so they prefer to just stay quiet instead.

## Shy vs. Reserved

Shyness means being uncomfortable with the presence of unfamiliar people. Yes, some introverts are somewhat shy,but they aren't all like that. They just don't like plunging in affairs of others when it's not necessary. They keep their selves reserved for essential things for important people in necessary situations.

## Unfriendly vs. Intimately Selective

It may be true that most introverts do not have that many friends, but that does not mean they are unfriendly. They look for long-term relationships.

Introverts do not close their doors to friendships, but they aren't capable of welcoming many people at once. They like to know someone gradually and create a solid foundation of friendship. F

## Depressive vs. Quietly Contented

Introverts are commonly mistaken as depressed people because they usually don't show their emotions. Depression is a mood disorder that causes someone to feel sad or lose their interest. Strong negative emotions affect their pattern of thinking and behavior. And introverts are far from being depressed.

Introverts are just quietly content within their own little world. They smile not because they want to toss a polite gesture when greeting people. They smile as a result of their satisfaction of something they've read, learned and appreciated. If an introvert vibrantly smiles at you, it's probably because you are someone they truly appreciate.

## Mentally Inept vs. Insightfully Intelligent

Many people underestimate introverts' intelligence because they don't usually hear them voicing out ideas, but the truth is, introverts have a fountain of well-constructed thoughts. Sometimes, they themselves consider their thoughts as being too abstract. They need time to simplify it by working with it alone first. Whenever their ideas pop out, they want to pay close attention until they formed those ideas into something doable.

Introverts have been present in many kinds of industry such as education, science, arts, showbiz, music and more. As a matter of fact, you will be meeting a few of them on the next chapter!

*"Sometimes life seems too quiet*
*Like a paralyzing silence*
*Like the moonless stars*
*Meant to make me strong"*


*Sorrow, Flyleaf*

# Chapter 3 - Famous Introvert Personalities

*"One of the strongest motives that lead men to art and science is escape from everyday life. A finely tempered nature longs to escape from the personal life into the world of objective perception and thought."*

*—Albert Einstein*

## FEW OF THE WORLD'S WELL-KNOW INTROVERTS

You do not really need to speak loud to make the world to listen. Some of the most well-known and influential people in the world were introverts. If you think you do not have anything to offer the world because you're an introvert, then gain inspiration from the following people who used their introversion to their advantage and became successful because they did.

## Albert Einstein, Physicist

For one reason or another, Einstein always had a hard time at school. His headmaster even told his father he wouldn't succeed in any career. When they moved to Italy, he continued to perform poorly at school and almost quit. Later in his life, he decided to become an electrical engineer and graduated in a school in Zurich, Switzerland, and that was the beginning of his significant contribution in the development of science.

The man behind the theory of relativity is often quoted as an introvert. Much of Albert Einstein's profound and abstract thinking is, no doubt, rooted from his introverted personality.

Albert Einstein is a great role model for people who are too scared to show off their introvert side. If you harness your introverted qualities, you may just be the next big thing in your own field.

**Barack Obama, US President**

Many people believe that the first African–American to become the US president, Barack Obama, is an introvert. His introverted style of leadership makes the US citizens to sit down and introspect for a while.

Before he pursued his political career, Obama was a teacher, lawyer and civil organizer. Despite his introverted nature, he remained a bold and skilled speaker. His ability to internalize problems, ideas and criticisms enabled him to leverage his extraordinary communicative capacities.This endearing characteristic of his made the people admire him even more, so much that they re-elected him in 2012.

## JK Rowling, Writer

Harry Potter is probably one of the most popular book series of all time.Even though the Harry Potter Series already ended, it continues to gain new fans.

The mind behind this remarkable novel series is none other than JK Rowling. She said that she came up with this idea while traveling from Manchester to London. On her website she wrote, "I simply sat and thought for four hours, while all the details bubbled up in my brain, and this scrawny, black haired, bespectacled boy who didn't know he was a wizard became more and more real to me."

Her wonderful writings also sparked the popularity of novel series. Some of these are Stephanie Meyer's "The Twilight Saga," Suzanne Collin's "The Hunger Games," and Veronica Roth's "Divergent." These books have been influential not just for book-lovers,but to typical people as well.

Introverts like JK Rowling didn't just believe in what they can do. They savored their intellectual journey. They have their own way of telling stories,and it capturedmany hearts around the world.

## Bill Gates, Microsoft co-founder and chairman

Before computers became easily accessible, Bill Gates already spent hours upon hours with it. His immense interest on computers led him to create Microsoft and develop the hugely popular Windows Operating System. Today, most of the computers in the world run on Windows. Even though there are many other operating systems available, many people still choose Windows because of its versatility and ease of use.

Because of his success with Microsoft, Bill Gates is now one of the world's richest people.He never let his bookish and quiet nature hinder him from pursuing his dreams and visions; instead he used them to his advantage.

## Mark Zuckerburg, Facebook founder

Facebook is currently the largest and most popular social media platform on the planet. Almost everyone in the world uses it. Facebook today is not just a meansto keep in touch with your friends and relations. It also became a place of advertisement, treasured memories, entertainment and self-expression. If it wasn't for Mark Zuckerburg's introversion, Facebook will not be what it is today.

## Allison Harvard, Top Model

You are not a real fan of America's Next Top Model if you don't know Allison Harvard. Although she didn't win the title of America's Next Top Model in both cycles she joined, Allison is one of its well-known contestants. Who could forget those big, round and blue doll eyes of hers? Who wouldn't fail to recall her odd fascination about blood and cats?

Allison is not just weird looking;she also behaves that way. Even though she keeps quiet in one corner while all the other girls are having fun, she cannot escape the eyes of the fans of the show. That's because she's not ashamed of her own brand of quirkiness. And that's what the world finds irresistible.

## Hayley Williams, Musician

Paramore's self-titled album received a lot of criticisms from fans and other musicians. Some says it's not the brand of music Paramore's known for, while others find it the mostexceptional among the albums they released. However, although they evolved differently from how they sounded before, Hayley's choice of words in constructing lyrics still breathes Paramore's original brand.

Even if Hayley Williams seems likea wild, energetic, angst-ridden vocalist, she has always been an introvert offstage. She's the kind of woman who's definitely into penetrating the mysteries of life. You can see it in her blogs and social media posts. You can reckon it in every rise and fall of her voice in their songs.

Her creativity and abstract thinking makes her go beyond from what's rudimentary to philosophical. That probably explains why some people find her as some kind of illuminati. But like other introverted musicians, her music just simply reflects her fascination towards the inner-world.

## Taya Smith, Worship Leader

Taya Smith is one of the current worship leaders of the Christian band, Hillsong United. For years, Hillsong has been the most popular band in creating phenomenal worship songs. Their music has been the theme song of the faith of numerous people around the world. If you have heard Taya Smith sing, you understand what they've been experiencing.

No one can ever tell just how introverted Taya Smith really is, but there's one thing for sure. Her quiet nature has never stopped her in living for something she exceedingly loves: singing for God. And this simple act of worship has touched the lives of millions and millions of people. It shone light for those wandering people in the dark. It brought hope and comfort to those living in fear.

## FROM THE HEART

Just like them, you can do remarkable things. You don't need to be outgoing for the world to notice you. All you need is a heart that never stops dreaming and a mind that never stops pondering.

Maybe introversion is something that's not widely accepted even in Einstein's generation, and that's the reason why he did poorly at school. But as he grew up, perhaps he knew it doesn't matter.

It's okay to be quiet. Nothing is wrong about having strange ideas. It's alright to be different. It's not going to make you any less human, in fact, it will even make you feel even more alive than you did before.

It demands a lot of staring at nothingness to come up with a wonderful story or a song. Tons of pondering is required to form creative ideas like Facebook and Windows OS. Quiet thinking is important to lead the fifty states of America. It takes a lot of silent moments to stop for once and wonder, "What can I do for the world?"

*"I don't know who I am anymore*
*Not once in life had I been real*
*But I never felt this close before"*

*This Close, Flyleaf*

# Chapter 4 - The Unique Blends

*"Your visions will become clear only when you look into your own heart. Who looks outside, dreams; who looks outside awakes"*

*—Carl G Jung*

Maybe you wonder why there are times you just want to explore aimlessly with your friends.You scream for unexpected night outs, road trips and thrillingescapades.Then there are moments wherein you just want to shut people out. Youyearn to be alone and enjoy the silence in a quiet beach, in an empty parking lot or simply in your bedroom. Perhaps this made you think that you're crazy; that yearning for silence and solitude is insane, but it isn't.

On the other hand, you might be uncomfortable with your own introversion. You feel odd and out of place. Being an introvert gives you the impression of being mentally ill. It drives you to want to "get out of your shell" and find a cure for being peculiar, but you couldn't find a way to do it, and if you did, it didn't feel right.

People congratulate you for finally "coming out of your shell", but the smile you put on is not the same as when you finishreading a well-crafted novel. It's not the same as when you have when someone spends time with you.You maintain the smile anyway because you think it's the cure for being an alien.

There is no cure for introversion at all. It's just a matter of embracing and loving that exceptional part of you.

## THE AMBIVERT FACTION

In the midst of introvert and extrovert scale, there are the Ambiverts. They are the people who have learned to stretch their selves from their introverted side to the extroverted. They know how to even out being quiet and being loud. On some weekends, they hang out on their own. And on some, they can party all night with the world. They can exchange in small talks but somehow finds it somewhat insincere sometimes.

However, Ambiversion is not something that comes naturally. The sole purpose of the introvert-extrovert concept is initially to ascertain whether a situation requires an extroverted or introverted response. Therefore, you have the choice in every situation whether you'll handle things inwardly or outwardly.

For example, if you need to work on an importantbook report, you need hours of solitude, blocking out any external stimulus and just get lost with your thoughts. On the other hand, if you need to present that report the next day, you have to consider external things like connecting with your audience and appearing interesting.

To sum this up, Ambiversion is something that a person learns as he grows older in life. It's either an extrovert learns to adapt introvert abilities or an introvert learns to adapt extrovert abilities.

## The Introverted Extrovert

"Introverted extroverts" are people who are dominantly extroverted, but acquired the abilities of an introvert. As they grew up, life taught them to embrace the value of solitude. They are still outgoing and like being in the company of their friends, but they learned just how to empathize, to be extra sensitive and to ponder first before taking actions.

## The Extroverted Introvert

In contrast, "Extroverted Introverts" are people who are dominantly introverts but acquired abilities of an extrovert. They are people who are willing to adjust to society, but they still need to be alone sometimes to recharge their energy.

## BLENDING IT

The world grew up in a society that blossom on interaction. Everyone finds fulfillment in having friends, regardless if you're an extrovert or introvert. Every human being experiences this extraordinary bond with others,but don't form these bonds mainly by interaction or by internal stuff alone.

When you love someone, it's not enough to justify what you feel and think about that person, you must act on your feelings too. On the contrary, plain actions are not enough; they must come from a deep meaning from within yourself.

To put it simply, as a human, you are neither a pure introvert nor extrovert. Life is not about creating labels based on how you do things. It's about doing things to create labels. Your distinctiveness doesn't deserve to be simply categorized under labels that society created.

You should only use the labels, like those that the Myers-Briggs Personality Test suggests, as a tool to know yourself better, but don't let them limit you from becoming so much more. You are special. You are exceptional. There are things that only you can do for this world and nothing, absolutely nothing, should be a hindrance to that.

*"And I'll let my heart go*
*It's somewhere down at the bottom*
*But I'll get a new one*
*To come back to the world that you've*
*stolen"*


*Monster, Paramore*

# Chapter 5 - Expanding the Limits

*"Being the odd one out may have its temporary disadvantages, but more importantly, it has its permanent advantages."*

*—Criss Jami*

Did you ever wonder why you tap your feet whenever you listen to a good music, or why you become teary-eyedwhen a certain part of a song moves your heart? It's amazing how something intangible can penetrate your soul. During moments you feel misunderstood, there's always music to let you know that in some place in this earth, someone understands.

When you listen to your favorite song, it makes no sense to say that the drums sound better than the guitar. Or the piano sounds better than the bass. Each instrument contributes to the beauty of the song.

The way howthe notesimpeccably blend with each other makes the song more than a song. It establishes a connection between you and the people behind the song that speech cannot even fathom. This is maybe because of what all of you encompass in common: afascination towards the inner-world. You share something that cannot be seen by the naked eye and only your soul understands. As Mitch Albom perfectly puts it, "Everyone joins a band in this life. And what you play affects someone. Sometimes, it affects the world."

## UPSIDES OF INTROVERSION

For a long time, people have been living in a hyper-outgoing culture. As people get more and more engaged with this extroversion hype, the more they get tired of chasing the fulfillment of life. This has set the world to explore and embrace the mysteries that introspection holds. People are convinced ofthe balance it can bring to the society. As they chose to embrace introversion, they gradually recognized the benefits it can give.

# The Benefit of Solitude

Life is full of stress. Majority of your week are spent with work or school. The endless to-do list robs you of sleep, relaxation and opportunities to have fun. However, if you strongly agree that life is not merely abouta series of finished tasks, then you must pay attention to the value of silence and solitude.

Solitude is a practice of being momentarily absent from the midst of other people and things so you can be alone with your thoughts and emotions. It breaks your "have-to-do-this" mindset by slowing your body down. Instead of burning a bunch of cash on therapy, just sit down in a quiet place and you'll experience the serenity your soul is longing for. By simply embracing your introversion, you are walking towards a life balanced by solitude.

Solitude disconnects you from the world for a while and bonds you deeply in your soul. By helping you create inner space, solitude clears the clouds in your mind so you can make wise decisions and unleash your creativity.According to research, most introverts have a habit of carefully thinking things through before acting. As you rest your soul in its tranquility, you'll become more self-aware, refreshed and self-disciplined.You'll have more value towards thoughtfulness, moral integrity and empathy for almost everyone around you.

## The Benefit of Discipline

Discipline is your way of making your choices, decisions and actions. If you ask successful people about their secret in achieving their goals, the answer would be proper discipline. You can dream high. You can envision a lot of possibilities, but if you ignore the value of discipline, you will not get anywhere fast.

Discipline cultivates a strong determination in you that will inspire you to do the things that you want. It gives you the nerve and confidence to face challenges and obstacles which form you in becoming a better individual.

Accomplishing things is much easier with time management. Discipline also yields a positive outlook in life. Staying well-ordered helps you work well thus keeps you away from draining tension. Live a life full of self-confidence and enthusiasm by being properly disciplined.

However, developing discipline requires plenty of inward reflections. To maintain your focus better, you need to converse constantly with yourself. There will always be distractions that will block your way and point you in a different direction. You have to keep reminding yourself which way you should go. Stepping inside the world of introversion takes you one step closer to a disciplined life.

## The Benefit of Creativity

Creativity is the ability to form new things or ideas. Imagination is what fired the world's development. Creativity is the reason for all of the modern conveniences you enjoy today and why many more are still coming.

Creativity is not just about arts and crafts. In one article in *Psychology Today*, Carlin Flora writes, "Buying into a limited definition of creativity prevents many from appreciating their own potential."

As you explore website blogs and YouTube blogs, you'll find many people posting DIY (Do It Yourself) tutorials about home décor, equipment, clothing tips, etc. It shows how much you can be creative about everything under the sun.

Being creative also gives a lot more payoffs. It generates balance and order in life by providing a sense of control over external things. As a result, it gives you a more positive atmosphere. It gives you a greater sense of comfort and personal growth.

Have you seen a child quietly enjoying his new set of crayons and coloring books? At first, you'll find it funny why a cat suddenly becomes violet, or a girl has green hair. However, as you watch how he was having fun coloring those images, you can sense the fulfillment on his face. This is because creativity enhances the spiritual and mental aspects of life. It makes thoughts and feelings more clear. And creativity can only be rooted from a healthy inner life.

Since longing for solitude is a natural habit for introverts, it gives them more room for creativity. Laurie Helgoe, author of *Introvert Power*, said that, "There's a lot of evidence that boredom is a precursor to creativity, and introverts are more welcoming of the solitude that engenders boredom."

## The Benefit of Strong Relationships

As mentioned earlier in this book, introverts are not anti-social. They just focus more on internal foundations of friendships that actually limits their friendliness.

Life is hard to imagine without the people you love around you. Without relationships, life makes no sense at all. Why do you have to pursue your dreams? Why would you even need to become better if it wasn't for the people you love?

By learning how to share internal things, like your random thoughts, emotional strugglesand confusions, you can create stronger relationships. By establishing strong relationships, you allow yourself to experience the real essence of being connected with other people.

*"I got a passion shut up inside my bones*
*My heart's about to bust*
*I'm bleeding hope*
*About to lose the truth and let it go*
*So radioactive*
*I'm a box matches"*


*Got that fire, Royal Tailor*

# Chapter 6 - The Introverted Road to Success

*"There is zero correlation between being the best talker and having the best ideas"*

—Susan Cain

## How to be a Successful Introvert

According to the first wide-ranging research study of the Myers-Briggs Type Indicator (MBTI) in 1998, 50.7% of the population is more inclined to introversion. And in a more recent study, the introvert percentage even rose up to 57.

Now, you might find this quite confusing sinceyour environment seems to be more extroverted. Or maybe introverts aren't just as noticeable as the extroverts, you guess. But, no. It's more likely that several of these introverts thought that putting off an extroverted façade will stop the endless misunderstanding. Perhaps they're thinking they'll succeed that way. But victory can't be conquered with that tactic. In fact, nobody has to fight introversion off.


To ensure a successful life, you must accept that your introverted side—no matter how small or big it may be—plays a dynamic role in your journey. From the previous chapters you have learned the real essence of introversion and the advantages it can give you. You have seen the lives of some people who succeeded, not "in spite of", but "as a result of" their introversion.Now, it's your turn to succeed in your own way.The following will be a set of advices on how to become a successful introvert.

## Embrace being an Introvert

Before doing anything else, strip down all your misconception about introversion and swim into your true colors. If you find it hard, keep reminding yourself that you are not alone. Half of the population is just like you. You can go to social media and find like-minded people as you. Many social media platforms are available out there.

Chatting with people similarto you will help you appreciate introversion more. The idea of talking to 20 people in a day might sound exhausting but with social media have made it easy for you. You don't even have to leave your room.

You can also inspire yourself with people who have already succeeded (like those mentioned in Chapter 3). Follow their steps and focus on how they kept being themselves without being thrown off by the extroverted world.

**Find your Passion**

Look for something you are passionate about. Do you love painting? Teaching? Writing? Music?Discover what activity makes you feel alive. Let yourself get carried away by your limitless imagination and strive to be excellent in the career you chose. Your passion will serve as the burning fire that will drive you to achieve your goals.

If Bill Gates didn't have his extraordinary passion for computers, Microsoft wouldn't exist. Maybe he thought it's something the world needs, and you should ask yourself that same question. What do you think the world needs? What breaks your heart? Can you do something to help? Are you interested enough to seek and pursue it?

Learn to be curious and follow wherever that curiosity may take you. Steve Job's curiosity led him to learn typography and develop design sensibility skills, and that paved the way for the birth of the iPhone.

Look for something that wouldn't just aid your financial needs, but something that you would want to do for the rest of your life even if you don't get paid to do it; that's your passion.

## Know your Strength and Weaknesses

Distinguishing where you are strong at and where you still need improvement is important to create an alleviated life. You have to understand your abilities.

Start by writing down the things you can and can't do. Ask yourself how and why you perform good or bad in that area. Next is to mirror your values; they will be your guidelines to approaching life. By identifying your values, you will know what things could be your strength or weakness to you, regardless of what it may infer to others. Examine if your actions align with your values, if they don't then reflect again. It would be better if you tell someone else about your values to force yourself to be accountable for your actions.

## Don't be Afraid to Socialize

There's nothing wrong with socializing because it will give you a wider range of people you can share your insights. If you find it difficult to socialize, there are certain techniques that will help make it a bit easier for you. You can start by copy-pasting social skills of some extroverts you admire. This doesn't mean that you're going to fake it or what, you just need to get some ideas how to start.

Next is to have control over the conversations during parties or group discussions. Avoid close-ended questions that can only be answered with yes or no. Try opening open-ended questions like "why do you think ____?" or "how is it that _____?" If it comes to the point that your energy is getting low, invite them to a low key place that may help you recharge (like a coffee shop, park, etc.). Learn how to make your worlds intersect and socializing won't be that much problem for you.

## Have a Consistent Quiet Time

Spending time with solitude may be hard to do today, especially if you've gotten used with a noisy and stressful environment. What you can really ensure for anoutset is to begin in small steps.

Try practicing solitude for five minutes a day. It doesn't have to be in a noiseless and human-less place at all. Five minutes of silence in your bedroom while everyone's still asleep is a good start. Or you can take a five-minute walk before you go to bed at night. Practice solitude as often as possible and you'll find yourself craving for more.

## Find a Safe Haven

If most people have dream houses, introverts have dream rooms. Having your own room will help you reenergize whenever you need to. Find a vacant room in your house and personalize it. Start by making a draft. Consider to include in your plan the things that will help you reenergize such as a bookshelf, dark curtains,a lamp (depending what kind of illumination is comfortable with you), and a comfortable chair.

If you don't have a vacant room in your house, find a nearby place where you can be alone. It can be a secluded bench in your local park or a far corner in your office's parking lot, a garden, a cemetery (this is creepy, but it works for some people), etc. Having your own private space will enable you to meditate. Just like the introvert facilitator of a meditation circle, Doug Imbrogno said: "Meditation allows you to not get swept away by the flood of thoughts and emotions, to sit by the side of the river, to watch the raging torrent and not get swept down."

In spite of where you wander during the day, always be reminded to take your mind with you. It's your fundamental private space. If your mind remains to free flow twisted thoughts, even if you are in the quiet place, it won't work. Take note of the things that feels right and what feels wrong. Make room for your desires. Try to always find clarity. Make improvements as necessary;exercise being straightforward with yourself,and most importantly, live a life full of love.

## Keep Journals

As you get used with being alone with your thoughts, more and more astonishing ideas will flood your mind. However, your mind is not like a computer hard drive,you just can't save everything that you like. It's important to keep journals by your side to record these enormous thoughts. Those can be something phenomenal someday.

If you're not a fan of pen and paper, you can download journal-writing applications on your smartphone. You can even make use of journals as a place for the unnecessary emotions that you find unhelpful in the process of your growth.

You should record important reflections because you will not get that many reminders about the things you learned the day before. Journals will allow you to revisit previous learning and enable you to assess what has been your progress up to the present.

## Think Outside the Box

Thinking outside the box sometimes means a little bit of craziness. Thinking outside the box requires creativity. And creativity empowers you to take the leverage of improvement higher. The more you move closer to improvements, the more likely you are going to succeed. From time to time, you need a changing perspective for you to see a problem or situation from different angles.

Some scientists, artists, architects, designers and others have the habit of observing and analyzing the nature to get inspirations. This has been a definitely fantastic strategy for people who want to think outside the box. By stepping into another world or another role, you will get many ideas that will aidat finding solutions to your problems. By being creative, you have the capabilities to offer something new to the progress of the world and the rest of humanity.

## Take the Lead

During the Global Leadership Summit 2014, Carly Fiorina said that everyone has the potential to lead. Global Leadership Summit or GLS anyway is a gathering of different kinds of leaders across the globe.

In that particular summit, Susan Cain was also one of the speakers.In her speech, she talked about the value of allowing your team to think in both introverted and extroverted ways. She said that you should allow people to have a few moments of silence to be alone with their thoughts before making group discussion. If there's a leaderwho understood the power of introversion so much, it's Susan Cain. Susan Cain is an introvert herself. She, in fact, wrote the book, "Quiet: The Power of Introverts in a World that Won't Stop Talking."

Leadership is not merely about bossing around flocks of people, but simply believing in what you can do. It's making people follow you by displaying how you love your life and yourself. If they witness the greatness of the path you're choosing, they'll follow your lead.

*"Gonna light it up like it's pyro*
*Gonna set it off and watch it explode*
*It's no secret*
*I know you feel it*
*We're coming alive"*


*Got that fire, Royal Tailor*

# Conclusion - Making It Matter More

*"Introverts are more effective leaders of proactive employees. When you have a creative, energetic work force, an introvert is going to draw out that energy better"*

*—Laurie Helgoe*

## LEADING PEOPLE TOWARDS THE BEAUTY OF INTROSPECTION

There are extroverts everywhere. You cannot escape them even as much as you wish you could.

It's okay to be friends with extroverts. It's okay to engage in small talk. They met you halfway so you should do the same for them. There are things that they don't understand about you and it's your job to make them understand. Who else do you think would, anyway?

Extroverts are not fan of guessing games. They focus more on what they see externally, remember? But you, as the more introverted one—or someone who understands introversion enough—can invite them to witness the beauty of contemplation. You don't need to push them to become one because a part of them already is. You only have to let them in in your own world of introversion. Inspire the little introversion living inside them and they'll figure it out themselves.

I hope this book was able to help you to understand what introversion really is. I hope this inspired you to embrace that introverted side of you. It longs for your attention for a long time.

The next step is to begin your journey towards success. Savor each thought-provoking moment, take pleasure with silence and marvelous concepts will come your way. Use those concepts in forming plans and share those plans with people you trust. Start making small actions in making those ideas into something real. Wait patiently until all you ever dreamed has become something world-changing or life-changing at least.

Finally, if you enjoyed this book, then I'd like to ask you for a favor, would you be kind enough to leave a review for this book on Amazon? It'd be greatly appreciated!


Thank you again for purchasing this book!